This

D0569344

I celebrated World Book Day with this
brilliant gift from my local bookseller,
Hodder Children's Books and Nadiya!

CELEBRATE STORIES. LOVE READING.

This book has been specially written and published to celebrate World Book Day.
We are a charity who offers every child and young person the opportunity to read and
love books by offering you the chance to have a book of your own. To find out more – as well as
oodles of fun activities and reading recommendations to continue your reading journey –
visit worldbookday.com

World Book Day in the UK and Ireland is made possible by generous sponsorship from
National Book Tokens, participating publishers, booksellers, authors and illustrators.
The £1 book tokens are a gift from your local bookseller.

World Book Day works in partnership with a number of charities, all of whom are
working to encourage a love of reading for pleasure.

The National Literacy Trust is an independent charity that encourages children to enjoy reading.
Just 10 minutes of reading every day can make a big difference to how well you do at school and
to how successful you could be in life. literacytrust.org.uk

The Reading Agency inspires people of all ages and backgrounds to read for pleasure
and empowerment. They run the Summer Reading Challenge in partnership with libraries,
as well as supporting reading groups in schools and libraries all year round. Find out more and
join your local library. summerreadingchallenge.org.uk

World Book Day also facilitates fundraising for:

Book Aid International,an international book donation and library development charity. Every
year, they provide one million books to libraries and schools in communities where children
would otherwise have little or no opportunity to read. bookaid.org.uk

Read for Good, who motivate children in schools to read for fun through its sponsored read,
which thousands of schools run on World Book Day and throughout the year.
The money raised provides new books and resident storytellers in all of the
UK's children's hospitals. readforgood.org

*€1.50 in Ireland

NADIYA'S

Bake Me a Story

Nadiya Hussain

illustrated by Clair Rossiter

Hodder
Children's
Books

HODDER CHILDREN'S BOOKS

First published in Great Britain in 2018 by Hodder and Stoughton

1 3 5 7 9 10 8 6 4 2

A CIP catalogue record for this book
is available from the British Library.

ISBN 978 1 444 94455 6
Export ISBN 978 1 444 94456 3

Edited by Emma Goldhawk
Designed by Alison Padley

Photography by Dan Annett and Adam Lawrence
Food styling by Shokofeh Hejazi and Lisa Harrison
Food photography by Joe Woodhouse and Georgia Glynn-Smith

Printed and bound
in China
Repro services by Imagewrite Ltd

The paper and board used in this book
are made from wood from responsible sources

Hodder Children's Books
An imprint of
Hachette Children's Group
Part of Hodder and Stoughton
Carmelite House
50 Victoria Embankment
London EC4Y 0DZ

An Hachette UK Company
www.hachette.co.uk

www.hachettechildrens.co.uk

Hello,

I'm Nadiya, and these are my three kids, Musa, Dawud and Maryam. It's very nice to meet you!

There are two special things that my family and I love to do together – sharing stories and baking. There's nothing we enjoy more than curling up with a book and having adventures in a new world.

Especially for World Book Day, I have put two of my favourite stories and the scrumptious recipes that accompany them into one book, so you can enjoy them too. You could read the story first and then make the recipe, or you could enjoy reading while your bake is in the oven. It doesn't matter which way round you do it – all that matters is that you have fun!

I really hope you enjoy this book, and that you find more stories to read next. You never know where your imagination might take you!

Nadiya

Musa

Maryam

Dawud

HELPFUL HINTS AND TASTY TIPS

Safety in the kitchen

Always make sure a grown-up is with you in the kitchen.

Don't touch the kitchen knives – they are sharp! If a grown-up says you can use them to chop or slice, be very careful.

Ask a grown-up to help you if you are using a food processor.

Always wash your hands in warm soapy water before you start.

Be careful of the hot oven and hobs.

Oven temperature

The recipes in this book have been tested in a fan-assisted oven. If you are using a conventional oven, increase the temperature by 20°C.

Measurements

g – grams
ml – millilitres
tsp – teaspoon
tbsp – tablespoon
°C – degrees celsius

Recipe guide

Each recipe has a guide to show you how easy or difficult it might be. Always make sure a grown-up is with you when you try any of the recipes, especially when it needs a knife or a food processor, or involves anything hot.

Beginner baker
– nice and easy

Clever cook
– a little harder

Little Red Hen and her
BREAD FRIENDS

Little Red Hen was best friends with

Big Brown Dog, Sleek Ginger Cat and Squeaky Black Rat. One sunny morning, Little Red Hen decided she would like to do some baking.

"*Will you come with me to buy the flour?*" Little Red Hen asked Big Brown Dog.

"*Not right now, Little Red Hen. I'm a little busy,*" said Big Brown Dog, and rushed away.

"*That's a shame. I will go and buy it myself,*" said Little Red Hen.

"*Will you help me find some baking powder?*" Little Red Hen asked Squeaky Black Rat.

"*Sorry! Got too much to do,*" said Squeaky Black Rat, and scuttled out of sight.

"*OK, I will find it myself,*" said Little Red Hen.

"*Will you help me get water from the well?*" Little Red Hen asked Sleek Ginger Cat.

"*Apologies. Now's not a good time,*" said Sleek Ginger Cat, and disappeared from view.

"I suppose I will get it by myself, then," said Little Red Hen. She was really confused. It wasn't like her friends to be unhelpful.

"Will you help me make the bread?" Little Red Hen asked them all a little later.

"Sorry, can't help," said Rat, Cat and Dog. And they all scampered off together.

"I shall make the bread all by myself," said Little Red Hen. "And then *eat* it all by myself, too," she added, grumpily.

Little Red Hen popped on her apron, lit the oven, washed her feathers and got to work. She was still a bit upset, so she gave the mixture a very enthusiastic stir.

Then Rat, Cat and Dog peeked around the kitchen door.

Little Red Hen pretended not to notice them.

"How's the bread looking, Hen?" they asked.

Little Red Hen pretended not to hear them.

Then the trio shuffled into the kitchen and presented Little Red Hen with a basket that was overflowing with fruit.

"SURPRISE!" shouted Rat, Cat and Dog. "We wanted to find you the yummiest blueberries and the juiciest oranges for your bread."

Little Red Hen was filled with joy. Her friends had done something lovely for her.

"Will you help me eat the bread?" asked Little Red Hen.

"We'd love to," said Rat, Cat and Dog. For Little Red Hen's blueberry and orange bread was famously delicious.

So the friends sat in the sunshine and shared the whole loaf. They rolled around laughing, their bellies full of sweet bread.

"What's better than best friends?" Little Red Hen asked Rat, Cat and Dog. "Bread friends, of course!

BLUEBERRY AND ORANGE
SODA BREAD

Makes one loaf

Ingredients

400g plain flour

2 tsp baking powder

½ tsp salt

50g caster sugar

2 tbsp light olive oil

100g dried blueberries

grated zest of 2 oranges

1 large egg

185ml buttermilk

Nadiya's tip

If baking with more than one child, the younger child could stir the mixture and the older child shape the dough into a ball

Method

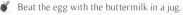 Preheat the oven to 180°C fan/gas mark 6. Line a baking tray with greaseproof paper.

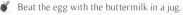 Sift the flour into a bowl, then add the baking powder, salt, sugar, olive oil, blueberries and orange zest and stir to combine.

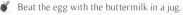 Beat the egg with the buttermilk in a jug.

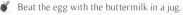 Mix the wet ingredients into the dry ingredients with a spatula, then gently bring the dough together by hand, to form a ball. Don't overwork it!

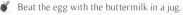 Place the dough on the lined tray and make two deep cuts on the top in a cross shape, nearly all the way through. Bake for 30–35 minutes, or until the loaf sounds hollow when tapped on the base.

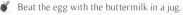 Remove from the oven and transfer to a wire rack to cool.

The Elves and the
CHOUX MAKER

Once upon a time there was a baker. He wasn't any old baker, he made the best choux pastry in the whole wide world. His choux was lighter, crispier and airier than any other baker could make, and people flocked to his bakery from far away just to get a taste.

He made long choux, short choux, round choux and even rounder choux. They were filled with every kind of filling and topped with every kind of topping you could ever dream of. But even though he was the best choux maker around, he was also the meanest. There were no free samples going at his bakery – not even at Christmas.

The baker's wife was quite the opposite. She was cheery and caring, and despite her husband's meanness, the kind-hearted woman still loved him very much. She would spend every afternoon in their flat above the shop, cooking the baker his favourite salmon curry for dinner.

One chilly December evening, as the baker was shutting up his shop for the night, a thin, scruffy man came into the bakery.

"I am looking for the famous baker who makes the world's best ch ... ch ... Sorry, how do you say it?"

"Choux. Like you'd say 'shoe'," the baker replied, sharply. He wanted to get home to his curry. "And that would be me you're looking for."

"Oh, great," said the man. "I don't have any money, but I am awfully hungry. I don't suppose you have a choux you could spare? Maybe I could take a couple for my friends at the shelter, if you are throwing out the leftovers?"

"Spare? You can only have the best choux in the land if you pay for it!" the baker growled, even though he knew he was just about to throw out the leftovers from the day. "If you don't have any money, go away, back to the shelter, where you belong!"

The baker pushed the man out of his shop and slammed the door.

Later that night, after the baker had finished his curry, his wife put on her coat and scarf.

"Where are you going?" he asked her.

"I cooked some extra curry for the people in the shelter. I'm going to drop it off," she answered.

"I don't know why you waste your time," he said, tutting.

"Because sometimes, people just need some kindness and a smile," she replied, and left him to be grumpy on his own.

It wasn't long before the baker, his belly full of the day's choux and a tasty portion of his wife's extraordinary salmon curry, fell fast asleep.

Meanwhile, downstairs in the bakery, something curious was going on. A gang of elves were sitting on the countertop, looking a bit puzzled.

"Are you sure this is the right place?" said one elf to another. "I mean, we're here to make shoes, right?"

"Yeah, that's what that pixie said, back at the crossroads," the other elf said. "World's Best Shoe Maker ..."

These little elves worked tirelessly to make shoes for those who didn't have any, especially over the winter when the cold would bite your toes.

"But where's the leather, or the tacks, or the laces?" a third elf asked.

"I haven't found any of that," said another elf from inside a cupboard. "But I have found butter, water, eggs and flour ... oh, and here's the World's Best Shoe Maker's instructions."

The elves followed the instructions as closely as they could, but as they took their shoes out of the oven, they were still perplexed.

"Do you think this is a new trend we don't know about?" said the first elf, trying on one of the freshly made shoes. They definitely kept his feet warm. He stood up to test them out on a walk, but he accidentally knocked a baking tray off of the countertop, sending it clanging to the floor.

The baker woke with a start and rushed downstairs, into the shop. "What are you doing in my bakery?" he shouted.

"Bakery?" the elves squeaked in surprise. "Isn't this the place where the best shoes in the world are made?"

"CHOUX!" the baker bellowed. "C. H. O. U. X! Sounds the same as 'shoe'."

Then the baker took a proper look at the elves with choux buns on their feet instead of shoes, and burst out laughing at the sight. He had not laughed in years. It felt good.

The elves joined in with the laughter, but it soon turned to worry.

"We have made all of this pastry, but now it's only going to go to waste ..." one elf wailed. "We are meant to be helping people, not wasting food."

The baker had an idea. He pointed at the elves. "You prick holes on the base of every choux and line them up. I will make a filling and a topping and then we can do something really special with them."

Back at the shelter, the baker's wife opened the door and gasped. Standing on the doorstep was her husband, accompanied by a gang of grinning elves, their arms piled high with cake boxes.

"Thought your friends here might like dessert," the baker said, gruffly.

The baker's wife pulled her husband into a huge hug, then they served the best choux buns to all the hungry tummies at the shelter.

The choux maker wasn't just the best choux maker in the world, he was now the happiest choux maker in the world, too.

SALMON AND GREEN BEAN CURRY

This is a delicious curry with lots of lovely spices to warm you from the inside out. It's easy to make and even easier to eat.

Serves 4

Ingredients

3 tbsp olive oil

3 garlic cloves, peeled and crushed

10g fresh ginger, peeled and finely grated

1 small onion, chopped

¼ tsp salt

1 tsp tomato purée

1 small tomato, chopped

½ tsp turmeric

2 tsp garam masala

400ml water

170g green beans, trimmed and chopped into 2.5cm pieces

450g salmon, skin removed, chopped into chunks

handful of fresh coriander, roughly chopped

Method

- Put the oil, garlic, ginger, onion and salt in a medium non-stick saucepan. Cook for about 5 minutes on a medium heat, until the onions have softened.

- Add the tomato purée, chopped tomato, turmeric and garam masala and cook for another minute.

- Add half the water and let it cook down until most of the moisture has evaporated.

- Add the rest of the water and the green beans, then cook for 5 minutes before adding the salmon. Cover and cook for 5 minutes on a medium heat.

- Take the pan off the heat and stir in the coriander.

- Serve with brown rice.

FIND THE WORDS

Can you find all the words hiding in Nadiya's wordsearch?

y	p	l	y	s	t	i	r
x	f	h	m	f	o	b	e
r	r	e	a	h	i	o	l
e	i	n	g	t	b	o	v
a	e	x	i	a	a	k	e
d	n	l	c	s	k	s	s
i	d	x	d	t	e	y	v
n	s	f	c	y	r	u	k
g	c	a	k	e	g	m	p

elves   friends   cake   hen

     baker   yum

          books   magic

tasty   stir   reading

SUPER SPOTTER

Look closely at these two pictures …
Can you spot **six** differences between them?

Answers: the stripes on the tablecloth have changed colour, there is an orange missing, there is a plate missing, the cat has a collar, the rat has changed colour and a basket of fruit has been added.

TASTY TANGLE

Who's going to get the delicious choux buns?
Will it be Nadiya, the elf or the baker?

SHORTLISTED FOR THE
BRITISH BOOK AWARDS 2017

OUT NOW!

NADIYA'S
Bake Me a Story

NADIYA'S
Bake Me a Story Festive

30 NEW RECIPES with original stories

'A wonderful gift for all aspiring bakers.' *Evening Standard*

'Brings families into the kitchen to spend time sharing stories and cooking.' *Gransnet.com*

'A host of easy-to-follow recipes for young chefs.' *Scottish Daily Express*

#BakeMeaStory

HODDER